when if ever alive

poems by

Kelly Alsup

Finishing Line Press
Georgetown, Kentucky

when if ever alive

Copyright © 2018 by Kelly Alsup
ISBN 978-1-63534-449-3 First Edition
All rights reserved under International and Pan-American Copyright Conventions. No part of this book may be reproduced in any manner whatsoever without written permission from the publisher, except in the case of brief quotations embodied in critical articles and reviews.

ACKNOWLEDGMENTS

Thank you to the following journals for original publication of some of these poems: *The Axe Factory* for "Central"; *Bombay Gin* for "fossil & found"; and *Fjords Review* for "Version".

The poem, "Righting Itself", is strongly inspired by William Carlos Williams' "The Red Wheelbarrow". "Golden Gate" draws inspiration from *Autobiography of Red* and *Red Doc>*, by Anne Carson.

Additionally, there are more loved ones, writers, and artists who have made my writing and life what it is than I will thank here, but I would like to offer special thanks to Qayyum Johnson, Sherri Marilena Pauli, Roy Blodgett, and Taj Hittenberger for the love and collaboration that have given sail to these works.

I would also like to thank Andrew Schelling and J'Lyn Chapman for inspiration, instruction, guidance, and kindness.

Publisher: Leah Maines
Editor: Christen Kincaid
Cover Art: Kelly Alsup
Author Photo: Kelly Alsup
Cover Design: Elizabeth Maines McCleavy

Printed in the USA on acid-free paper.
Order online: www.finishinglinepress.com
also available on amazon.com

Author inquiries and mail orders:
Finishing Line Press
P. O. Box 1626
Georgetown, Kentucky 40324
U. S. A.

Table of Contents

Incline 1

Golden Gate 2

Growth Rings 4

what would you do for 5

Mosaic 9

The One 10

Migration 11

ballistic 14

your topography of 15

Redd 16

(Blue) 17

Central 18

Western Tanagerism 19

Righting Itself 20

false endings 21

fossil & found 22

Version 23

California Poem 24

Matera 27

Alight 28

Agrigento 29

After that, ... 30

for my family and friends
                    and the ocean of creation we swim in

Incline

The place I've found is neither
comfortable nor disquieting,

and I wonder if each place
is as good as the next.

I linger here beneath laurel leaf fingers
in a pool of discarded gloves—

a spooky lava, as when young,
we scattered the sofa's coarsely upholstered cushions
across the basement floor,

dare not touching the molten mayhem
just inches below our leaping.

What duff and litter scare me now? And how do I take grown steps
directly through the fractured leaf fall?

The delicate new growth sprouting,
the hound's tongue panting blue and happily

and many trios of resinous leaves
that appear to signal of crossing with

only gentlest care,
or again, not at all.

Then, another triune—this one of joggers scuttling crisply

over the embankment
with black tails down
and large ears learning,

always learning, whether to continue
on a chosen course—

how faith is found when everything seems
further up trail than expected.

Golden Gate

If I were Anne Carson, I'd write about two good people biking out together on a bridge. The two, their names would be something like Dolphin Eyes—gray in hers magnetizing the slippery cetacean ahover and muscle in the heaving current—and Green Shoes—like the apple of his bookshop and the algal way it bundled sunlight, giving him air to breathe. Her eyes couldn't see clearly past mammal; his shoes zigged and zagged him up and down the blocks as another language, wondering however fulfillment.

The bridge, completely companionable, also felt lonely, not for its coeternal color or paired cantilevers and towers but for the way a bridge both binds two things together and dignifies their separation.

So she finned a false euphemism to mask her desire to once again feel his nimble mouth on hers. For her own mouth to irresist like popcorn kernels shattering in dance of suction, tongue, lift, and the jaw-loose pistons of rhythm teeth, radiantly breaking after brackish lips.

The way the light shone on the surf past the bridge's lamp-made shadow, the moon a milder turtle on its back, shell become milk unspilled, swelling, living its home a cup of sake wine instead of the familiar covering.

Green Shoes toeing the seedbed of stars.

Dolphin Eyes blinking the moment she felt she had hands, one finger finding a soft little spot where heavy head meets the outstretched neck with its tiny antennal hairs and drop of ear silken & water-whispery.

& his long, capable hands, they reached, too, in the span between weight they each could bear and the place where those anchors are ringed by dream, by mutable, somehow stabilizing ocean.

Growth Rings

I remember, years ago, my first times lying with men. Sometimes
I would not wear underwear, and this discovery would be the thing

that excited them—or maybe it would be my narrow belly, a smooth lake
where they could lap. Sometimes I would feel shy of my small breasts,

but other times I was fearless as a warrior—with steel eyes, I surrendered
my spear-tip nipples, unreservedly succulent. Things I enjoyed about them:

broadness of chest, flatness of nipple. Roundedness of shoulders. The place,
of course, where pubic hair begins, darkly—most earthen of browns and

raven-black, bristly nests. To hold them now, I am not sure
I can delight as much, for all the freshness my eyes had then. Each person's

unique structures like first-held vistas in foreign countries. And, I'm not so sure
that revealing the moon-slopes of my thighs or burls of my buttocks, rich

for climbing, would now fulfill as much bravery as it once did. But I do suppose
there is still the matter of what I hold inside—the phloem that descends

from the top of where I have gathered all water—
and drips, cleanly, at my roots, where slick snails make loose

my joints and heat many layers of what has fallen. And the xylem that
retrieves it, bending accelerated nerves up through my trunk and its vessels,

curling my limbs and voyaging from my throat,
its brightest feathers in fertile song after song after song after song after song—

what would you do for

i. EARTH

Sharp & sensitive. Both these aspects of mind have gotten the better of me the last some years. Though not the best. Snow an apparition. Someone's wearing agreeable perfume. It's important the soap dispense more immediately than love. A surfactant floats on water, easier to understand. If I don't take us to the depths, no one will. It is always my tectonic plates skidding out, grief measured on a Richter scale of lost hungers. Maybe if we allow ourselves to be sad, we'll stop devouring each other & begin combing through the long strands. Let's make bones of the billboards.

ii. AIR

There's a bird singing from a sunny pine bough; it manages to get my attention. These pines that live wherever I go, and the birds speaking luminous language. Does sun in firewall strategy engage or generous a balterous dance continue? Friends call the words *ungrounded, uprooted.* The radish, turnip, or—egads—lettuce start thinned from soil packet. But in my hands, the rubies bleed perfectly, hardened pits whistling for loft to somewhere rougy blossoms, after torrents of rain, gravitate toward expansion. Bright red fox saunters by, survived, gallops up the road. And the world goes bronchial. Grows into right timing.

iii. WATER

Location of memory, an active act. Every time we do something, working from memory or making it anew. *I regret to inform you the plastic bag in the field is not an egret.* Act of looking at shapes recalling memories of egret, while upon closer looking, hatching new memory of litter—how it's bound to be out there if we lay it. Not unlike memory. Senses sincere, nonetheless sure to see what we've seen *before, then* anything else our collective actions plume at rapid spring through a reedy, blue-green door that's hinged on the egress of mercury from the body.

iv. FIRE

A few thrusts of tears as though time before rising were built of ice crystals made ready for sun's first glint. Retrieve gooey pearls around yesterday's mascara splashes. Slice orange, slice apple, star and moon, peanut butter and salt for ploughman. Neighbor's Chocolate Lab on roof again—not shaman's vision but real, and the sun sparks affectionately on his coat as he pullulates, lees, flashes. He's okay—doesn't melt. They bark him in or he wills himself. In, then down, out to the fragrant yard where thaw is early beginning & force under frozen streamtop has been keeping everything alive.

Mosaic

I am something like the aquatic caddis, who crafts a small rock shell to protect its bones—I have broken three in my legs alone, along with a tiny toe; it went back in time on the face of the clock about one-and-a-half hours, my feet curling over themselves, an ardent runner fainting from dehydration. Of the four, two bones were sacrificed to heat; the others to water. All were stitched anew, just as my outlook, and resilience, and the sun swath around this landmarked skull grew. The seals and their coal-black eyes say *wait, stay there, don't come any closer,* but sentinel knows how each mottled flake of blubber disperses by slick glance of soap. You can be glad for your moments of submarine refuge, a glued-back-together orbit of rubble. But fire and flood are both here, again, and you need to kick that casing. You were born into those legs
for swimming,
                as well those jointed limbs,
                              grafted,
                                          extend to land and embark—

The One

Nodding toward the future, the chestnut Arabian, keratin-hooves searching forward, like dust is not actually meant to be settled, or as heaviness in the foot will generate ricochets in between smooth-gaited moments. Veering ever-over the bark eucalyptus that flails in the rainstorm, little child, but whispers—*open the road of experience*—recollected, the matter of whether the flash is precognition having finally entered, whereas prior, only one quarter your horsepower invested in acceptance; now, the past canters up to the galloping present; a yearling lightnings its legs till they thunder, yearning for the colt. Understand: even animals need alone time. M-Make your missteps count.

Migration

i.

Strawflowers flame out in bristly petal—
red pepper jelly, papaya & autumn
lake light at sunset or sunrise—in childhood
water moved little; now high tides and low tides.

You run the tiller, just beyond succulent
flowers magenta that palette the fog with
something starbright—puffs of milkweed down &
other distinctly dispersing streams are aquake

in the pleasure of dangling, having
formed, burst open, and bearing wings.

ii.

)I(adjust my eyes as they pepper about
upon mallow, sorrel, speedwell & chickweed.
Today the sandy flats of your garden,
tomorrow the salty slopes of mine.

)I(wear a bracelet you bought for me—
unfamiliar tree nut seeds in colors
not unlike the ones that draw your eye
to pick for me & the sky that always holds us.

)I(rest on you my turquoise beads
a frightening & beautiful surf. Monarch
skin drops back, their fulcrums to be slaked
& ringed, jetties solid in purpose of vulnerability.

iii.

when numbers decreased, the people looked higher
  to where the tallest shoots of the tree had grown

                and so, the tallest nectar

                symmetry of embered fans
                    and charcoal lines
                      their link to soil—

                          our veins carry
                          the minerals
                          same

                                          the long, tenuous highways

ballistic

And what of love can be teased from a garden—
soaked in sure sun & retaining of mineral?
The henbit nettle conceals its curative
concepts through its commonness. The kale,
tapped here and there by fruit petals, keeps
the secret of winter calmly and grows sweeter
for its temperance (loyalty). A mower fires up &
dies back down in a clatter of high grass & wood chip.
If only someone weren't tending the machinery, I wouldn't
listen as carefully as I can to the wind tunneling through the
bittercress siliques, lemon balm, dock, blade, thistle, and allium.
Now a mating pair of finches gold, rustle of brassica stalk in bloom,
and mason bees russet fuzz over the field, our valves of perception feel
where hunger carries us on and rises from flowers where that feeling grew—

your topography of

topography of your
features begins to press
and fit into me
as words make places
over a grid
letters emboss upon
the paper

color
not so much applied
as filling
in the spaces, being
drawn out of
an unrelieved landscape

water, first frozen, routing
exposure of
minerals, then melting
gravity
over new
surfaces, brand new
surfaces, literally created
& no sooner coming forth with
the richness of what's been buried for
thousands of years behind and ahead, turned stones in the creek
bed flashing, scales of fish, come in from the ocean—it's about time

Redd

The morning the black cat's soft paws ratcheted all down the dock to our front porch pumpkin; times that a harbor seal tracked me in bay-brack, having translated my turbid wake into diction with its whiskers; and one day, a lone sea otter, looking ever the otter, all abackfloat, feet like flags and head telescopic. Nourishment's lures motion us to water, then signal us back to shore the same. Prolific urchin, herring of unscripted color, things that twitch or do not but blaze just as though. Fruit and flicker, the flirt of nasturtium flower, red made of smoke like forest fire and a periodic table of minerals aflame, heart of what was left upstream scaled in blush.

(Blue)

I found a robin's egg—you know the color—humid midwestern summer day, hint of green—I thought—what if I can save it? If / I can save it, I must, but I was still / working around the garlic & lettuce, skimming back grass with a spade, raking out tilled in beds for better germination. / I placed the egg in the shade for later / under the Spanish lavender //

In the evening, when those purple flags were touching / the sky like water color / I went back to pick up the embryo, all / folded beneath the calcified chamber //

But it was gone. In its place, a hole / of similar size / where lateral muscles / of serpentine swagger / must have had //

Other plans—

Central

Not coffee but bobcat. Lynx rufus californicus. I saw it, a chubbier, fluffier one than of summer. And when I say chubby, I really mean squat. And full. Full of fur like our Lynx Point Siamese cat. Squat as in not so much living its litheness as slinking through life with this gravity-guidance.

It paused within fifty feet of the chickens. Its posture upon being spotted was squatting, which means it watched us before we saw it perusing its diurnal options. Then back-padding, down toward coastal scrub and a raucous ocean. And hopefully a rabbit, and a cozy rock crevice or hole in the Monterey cypress.

Western Tanagerism

                                          They killed another
                              chicken at the Kitchen & another

one at Salt. Pork
also cures well, and bright birds

                                                 carry their shadows
                              under and over the fault. Mean

while Venus sears her light
through the window, my belly burns

                                              with all creating & all
                                  that swirls uncreated, but for

            the red

                      // red markings of its way //

Righting Itself

whether next desire embrace
depends so much
under feathers

the dust-fume silica slicing
every fastidious
red haunt—

diatomaceous earth, seafloor
harvest brought to surface
gently

silting the sacred
quivers, the inverted

trust
of the sentient

quill

.

false endings

The first burn-off of fog is a fake-out. I take my sweater off but want to put it back on—at least at first. Then I let cool puffs of air brush my skin, while gray water froths at the mouth like a whale when it sieves out water but keeps all the tiny krill. Pelicans do this also—let liquid drain out of their throat pouches, gallons at a time, before sliding the herring down *for one last thrill*. Or so I jest. I ingest my own fill of meats, not wanting to kill so much as feed. But in order to feed ourselves, that which we harvest must be fed somehow—some little scraps of gratitude, some clean breaths, waste for turning & transmuting—an assimilable amount that breaches attention and baleens the sky & sparkle-hatched water back to cerulean blue.

fossil & found

each heart its own organism
a cat, cloyed belly up by its tender
kill, an impulse to conquest as well as
to feed: light-footed threads of territory
shuffling into dust, or is it clay, the draft of
wing or the space the water will always move
between, without being noticed, almost except
when it has been dry for—oh, what—a few days
& a rainstorm or seaswell enfolds what once was held

by shell & soft meat will wound no more
by salt, by birth, by wave unfettered
ring after ring of music

a coral place
a red reef of gold
a silver sheaf where what is

coiled and unbound all oxidize blue
latches, hinge of spine snapped open to face
a threatless sky, maker of which this old & sauntered
sedimentary rubble assembles a ground we are known by

Version

The plane must pass through winter air
Pedals and paddles are only as strong as

Seed to crown, seed to crown
Do not lose track of the train as it tempers

Lose, lose: some sound, some silence
Hear the timbre when something rings you

When someone rings you, grab your nametag
Scratch the addresses that do not hold you

Like waves before you, change the lines
You were before the breakwater knew you

California Poem

Surrounded by quiet,
curling oaks,
and laurel leaves
with their single paintstrokes,
green upon green collage
of lime and olive, or lime
flesh in the sun
and dark lime rind, or olive
fruit and its oil.

And a thin
carpet of newsprung grass
also green, young celery
green of so much that succeeds
first in sun, between dry fallen
oakleaf that makes
the greening below
possible, and the greening
above more noticeable,
as it comes.

California
I have come to know
by season—know
and love. Not to forgo
other places, but to admit
a slow commitment to
the chaos &
inheritance here—
continuity of rock & oak.

And fragrant
features of laurel unfastening
the feeble buttons of time.

And always the new
outcrops of grass,
temporal,
to be grazed and trampled
and shaded and browned.
Then again.

I marvel at once,
then feel the earth shift,
hear the sibilance of tires
behind the delicate
and sometimes insistent
birdsong. What question
do I even have
for the scarcely
budding oaks
draped in moss?
It seems I cannot speak it.

There is want to live fully
and deeply, and who am I
to say that such roots
and leaves
do not wait here? For
it would be a lie.
And lies do not
a poet make.

And yet the sirens I hear
go also to help
somewhere I cannot see.
And the golden light
on my hair as it dangles
in front of me, notebook
on bluejeaned thigh
on cool, composed rock—

the golden light
disappears within hours
and I will walk on
from this ringed spot,
small flecks of humus
on the treads of my shoes.

Matera

It was time to reconstruct the city,
so everyone left town.

There were big machines and small machines
and the stone that had always been there for

to shape a humble beauty and stronger face
and bring new life to the ramparts.

When enough light had entered
and the footholds paved anew,

the rooster crowed once more and people set out—
not to define a border but to find the center where

the cobbler hammered and bread
in a kiln bore a name.

When the villa's ardor emerged,
arose tiny sculptures and came modest apertures

all around—small stamps against the clamber
to rule high above in a tower.

Be it religion or riches, there is no canal
from which we do not all drink.

For a spoonful of water, I will bang my tambourine
and gather bell beans for tomorrow.

Alight

Outside the town is a common veranda
where clutch of eggs and basket of fennel shared.

The white rooster's tail like an angel's wing ascends
and in its wake glitters down a whisper.

Instinctual joy, a saluting red comb
reminds the flock to listen.

Agrigento

To shear and rake the bramble is to open up the heart.
Each leaf that shades the bud partakes a lion's share of sun.

If horns are brought to battle, then, a hand will capture their force.
The weather rains down on everything, the blossom before the fruit.

The fruit before the nut is burrowed through in search the beginning of time.
Pet any sweet hound except the one who guards the skin of truth.

You can graze your sheep in the orchard, but better not your goat.
Yet if you want your garden cleared, the goat, with spired horns

        toward heaven, is your caring beast.

After that,

there's a crescent moon with a yellow shroud
the color of honeyed hair

and Venus a wheat field, red through which
you part the stalks to find your way

to me in a place where grain is threshed
as a horse swats flies
with its tail

to create separation
from one incarnation
to the next

A graduate of the University of Oregon and Naropa University's Jack Kerouac School, **Kelly Alsup** works from coastal California where she gardens, teaches, dances, swims, and sings. Born in California and raised in Nebraska, her writing can be found in *The Axe Factory, Bombay Gin, Buddhist Poetry Review, Fjords Review,* and *Inverness Almanac.*

www.ingramcontent.com/pod-product-compliance
Lightning Source LLC
LaVergne TN
LVHW041505070426
835507LV00012B/1348